This book is dedicated to the owners and staff who act as custodians of these great houses for the pleasure of future generations

The Treasure Houses

of

England

A View of Eight Great Country Estates

·

Photographs by
Earl A. Beesley and Garry Gibbons

Introduced by
The Duke of Marlborough

VIKING

VIKING

Published by the Penguin Group
27 Wrights Lane, London W8 5TZ, England
Viking Penguin Inc., 40 West 23rd Street,
New York 10010, USA
Penguin Books Australia Ltd, Ringwood,
Victoria, Australia
Penguin Books Canada Ltd, 2801 John Street,
Markham, Ontario, Canada L3R 1B4
Penguin Books (NZ) Ltd, 182-190 Wairau Road,
Auckland 10, New Zealand

Penguin Books Ltd, Registered Offices:
Harmondsworth, Middlesex, England

First published in Great Britain by Viking 1989
1   3   5   7   9   10   8   6   4   2

A CIP catalogue record for this book is available from
the British Library

ISBN 0–670–82879–3

Frontispiece:
Morning Mist, Castle Howard

Designed by Beesley Gibbons Ltd
Colour separations by Culver Graphics, UK
Typeset by Adsetters Ltd, UK
Printed in Spain by Cayfosa, Barcelona.

Contents

Foreword by the Duke of Marlborough

If there is one single word which sums up the importance of the English country home, it is this: heritage. The heritage of over 900 years of noble history. The heritage which is the birthright of every occupant of the British Isles.

The Treasure Houses of England is a celebration of that heritage. Through images and words it seeks to capture the mood and atmosphere of these magnificent residences, the perfection of their settings, and that quite unmistakable aura which marks the solemn passage of years.

The architectural and decorative richness of the English historic house is unparalleled in the rest of the world, presenting an imposing grandeur matched only by the grace employed by its architect. Yet beyond the bold lines and symmetry there is so much more that often remains unheralded: the sweeping parklands of each estate, the historical relevance of each edifice, and the collected art treasures and artefacts that are housed within those walls. It is a combination of these unique features which offers us a vital, living link with our past.

If, as I have said, **The Treasure Houses of England** is a definitive celebration of our heritage, it must be added that it is also a tribute to the owners of these magnificent estates. It is only through their unflagging efforts that these houses have retained their importance and stature in the modern world. We must never forget that this heritage is our birthright, an integral part of our English way of life.

The historic properties which make up the Treasure Houses of England group are all fine examples of England's history. Most are still the homes of the families who have lived in them for generations. The group first joined forces in 1975 when they launched a 'co-op with a difference'.

The contribution which these historic houses make to Britain's tourism reflects the tremendous popularity of our fine heritage, and the deep curiosity and desire of the majority of visitors to know how the great aristocratic families lived. As a group we see ourselves spearheading the attack to bring the stately homes of England to the attention of visitors from all over the world.

This book provides the reader with a unique pictorial view of these eight great estates. The photographs have been taken throughout the four seasons in varying light, which means that the subjects are constantly and often dramatically changing within the landscape.

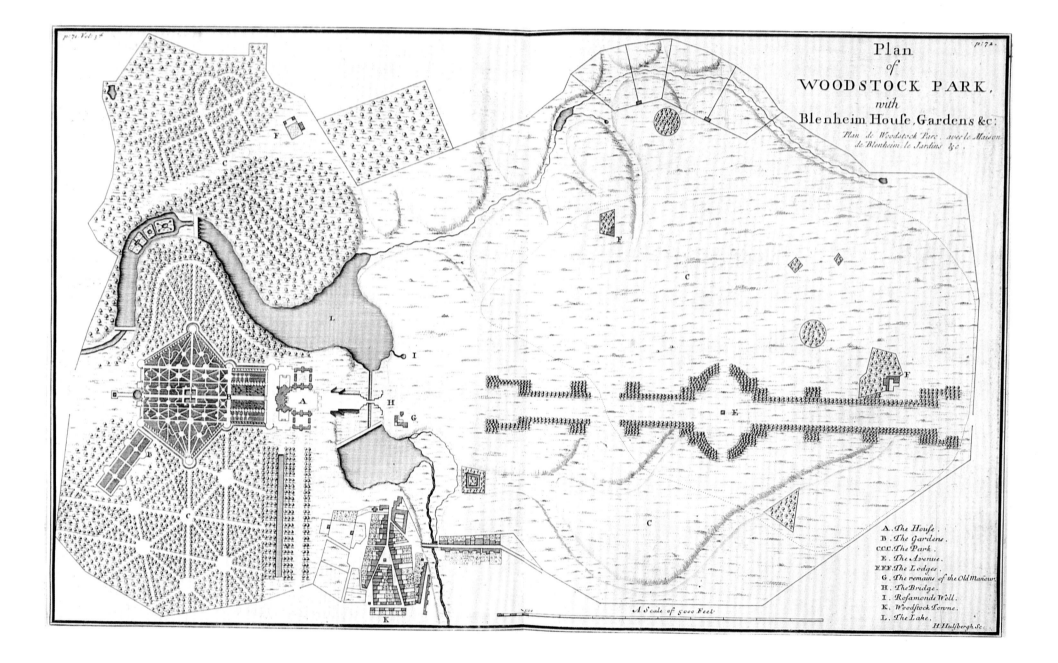

Plan
of
WOODSTOCK PARK,
with
Blenheim House, Gardens &c:

Plan de Woodstock Parc, avec le Maison
de Blenheim, le Jardins &c.

A . The House .
B . The Gardens .
CCC . The Park .
E . The Avenue .
FFF . The Lodges .
G . The remains of the Old Manour .
H . The Bridge .
I . Rosamonds Well .
K . Woodstock Towne .
L . The Lake .

A Scale of 5000 Feet .

H. Hulsbergh Sc.

Woburn Abbey

WOBURN ABBEY

•

*Woburn Abbey has been the ancestral home of the Dukes of Bedford since
1547, when it was confiscated from the Cistercian monks and given to Sir
John Russell, later 1st Earl. The house was restored and given a Palladian
façade by Henry Flitcroft in the mid eighteenth century and was later
remodelled by Henry Holland in the 1790s. The 3,000-acre park was
landscaped by Humphry Repton in 1804. The Abbey is now the home of the
Marquess of Tavistock, heir to the Duke of Bedford, and his family.*

Introduction by the Marchioness of Tavistock

My favourite time of the day is the early evening, when the house is closed
and most of our visitors have gone to their homes. The park is very
peaceful then; the sun sets behind Basin Pond and with that reflected in
the water and the deer, who always come down at that time of night,
grazing in front of the house, it makes a truly idyllic scene.

The building isn't as dramatic as Castle Howard or as cosy as
Haddon, but it has its own character and the best view of the house, I
think, is from the south-west, where you see the combination of Henry
Flitcroft's west wing and Holland's south wing. This is part of the route I
like to take when I am out riding, which, sadly, isn't often, as there always
seem to be so many things to organize and so many people to talk to
about the running of the house and the estate.

I must admit that I wasn't very pleased when I heard we were
moving to Woburn in 1974. Neither Robin nor I had ever expected to be
here – we always thought it would pass to our eldest son, Andrew – but
that is an old story now. Both of us have become very attached to Woburn
and I think have shouldered the responsibility very well, and we have
been very happy until Robin suffered a major stroke here last year. But he
is an amazing person with such strength and is now on the way to
complete recovery. I have been very lucky with the support and love I
have had from my sons, all my friends and the people who work for us on
the estate. Without that, life would have been very difficult.

Robin's family have lived at Woburn since the seventeenth
century (although it was willed to them by Henry VIII in the sixteenth), so
it has always been a family home. I can remember as a young girl coming
to Woburn with Robin, and one day walking through the rooms he
turned to me and said, 'You'll live here one day, Henrietta'. I remember
standing there and looking at all the apparently vast rooms and thinking,
'No, never'. Jamie, our youngest child, is the only one of our sons to have
been born here – he was one of the conditions I made that I would live at
Woburn. Andrew and Robin were born at Chevington Russell, our lovely
Georgian house near Newmarket, so they don't have quite the same
attachment to Woburn as Jamie does. But the whole family do feel this
total commitment now to Woburn and we regard ourselves very much as
the custodians of our children's heritage.

My husband has embarked on an enormous restoration plan which
will take many years to complete. At the moment we are restoring the

west front. The house was faced in Totternhoe Clunch and given a Palladian façade by Flitcroft in the 1750s. Unfortunately this is a rather soft sandstone which has not weathered well, and coupled with the pollutants in the air (there are brickfields not far away), erosion has taken place. So we are having to cut back some of the stone, replace the quoins, and where necessary replace with fresh stone. The costs are astronomical and the incomings cannot possibly cover the outgoings. Luckily, as Woburn is a listed building, we have managed to get a small grant from Government funds.

There are so many drains on our resources, not only the fabric, but also the contents which must be maintained and restored where necessary. Then there is the 3,000-acre deer park, the roads and Chambers' Bridge, due for complete restoration, the wall, over twelve miles of it around the park, and the forestry department. We plant approximately 100-200 trees each year to replace those lost in the gales and by natural wastage. There are a series of lakes in the park fed by underground streams, with amusing names like Shoulder of Mutton and Basin Pond, on which the 4th Duke kept a fully manned twelve-gunned frigate during the mid-eighteenth century when he was First Lord of the Admiralty. I have never been able to discover how it arrived – it must have been transported by road – but what fun to have your own boat to play pirates on and to sound off a salvo when the spirits are high.

One of the exciting things about Woburn is that you never know what you may find next. The other day I discovered a really beautiful Sèvres plate, part of a dinner service made for Marie Antoinette, hidden away in the back of a cupboard where it had lain undisturbed for years. I enjoy planning the redecoration of the house, choosing the wall hangings and the fabrics. I have a good eye for colour and can carry a specific colour in my mind until I find the right match. We have our own maintenance staff and decorators and they are very patient and long-suffering, especially when I make them produce card after card of colour samples until we hit the exact one. I think they get a great feeling of satisfaction when the job is done, at least I hope they do. The furniture and pictures are chosen from the collection, so the room displays are never static, although some items come from the storerooms. There are a lot of surplus pieces of furniture and pictures which have to be stored carefully; some of them came from the other houses which we sold for death duties, and some from the east wing which was pulled down in 1950. I suppose one of these days a future generation may consider rebuilding the east wing.

Robin is also very involved with the golf course and club, which he planned shortly after we arrived at Woburn. It is in a beautiful setting not far from the Abbey and has become one of the most important golf courses in England. The Dunhill Masters is played there every year, and the Ford Ladies' Classic, plus many more, and all the great golfers have played there.

The family have always been great innovators, starting in the late sixteenth and early seventeenth centuries with the fen drainage scheme. The 5th Duke, my husband's favourite ancestor, had his agricultural shows and experimented with new breeds of sheep; he was also rather radical in his views and a supporter of the revolution in France. The 9th Duke patronized the first experiments with electrically powered engines when he acquired a tender for his yacht, the *Northumbria*. My favourite of Robin's ancestors must be Mary, the Flying Duchess, a lady with a multitude of interests: nursing (she built a cottage hospital in Woburn village in 1898), aviation (she set records for flights to India), ornithology, fishing and painting – and in 1905 she learnt the art of ju-jitsu. I wish I could have known her. I have just finished redecorating a room where I have hung some of her collection of watercolours of cottage gardens and Thorburn animals. The room is named after a small estate she once owned in Sussex, called Wispers.

Living at Woburn and knowing its history and its family, who have contributed so much in the past to politics, philosophy, art and horticulture, has made me conscious of a desire to contribute something extra besides the duty of looking after Woburn, the estate and the people who work here. In 1965 I bought our first filly foal, and the Bloomsbury Stud, named after one of the Bedford estates in London, was born, and is now based at Woburn. Then I told Robin I would try to make his family's racing colours famous again – the 5th Duke had bred three Derby winners at Woburn in the 1780s and 1790s. Ten years later I bought dear Mrs Moss, who has become something of a legend in her lifetime. She has produced ten individual winners and has three sons at stud – Precocious, winner of the Gimcrack Stakes, Krayyan and Jupiter Island, who won the Japan Cup in Tokyo in 1986, breaking the track record. Thanks mainly to Mrs Moss, I have started to achieve what I set out to do, and the once famous purple and cream striped colours with the black velvet cap and distinctive gold tassel have been carried with success. Maybe this year, the bicentenary of the 5th Duke's horse Skyscraper winning the Derby, we may have a Classic victory here at Woburn and I too will have brought something extra into the family's heritage.

Illustrations

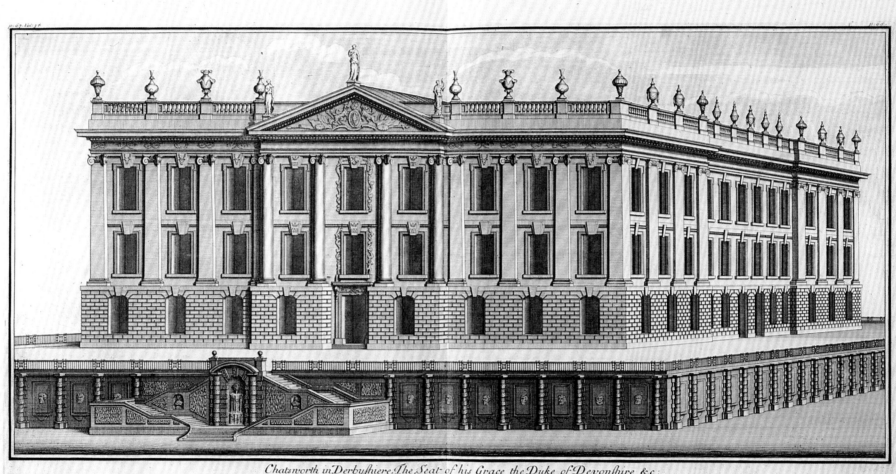

Chatsworth in Derbyshiere, The Seat of his Grace the Duke of Devonshire &c.
Chatsworth dans de l' Comté de Derby Maison de Duc de Devon.

Ca: Campbell Delin: H. Hulsbergh Sculp:

CHATSWORTH

•

*Chatsworth, the Derbyshire seat of the Dukes of Devonshire, was originally
built by the formidable Bess of Hardwick and her husband Sir William
Cavendish from 1552 onwards. Their descendant the 1st Duke rebuilt the
house, and Sir Jeffry Wyatville added a huge wing for the 6th Duke.
The park was remodelled by Lancelot 'Capability' Brown and the estate
covers over 13,000 acres.*

Introduction by the Duke of Devonshire

Chatsworth has two roles: it provides a home for those who work here and it attracts hundreds of thousands of visitors each year. It is my job to see that these two different aspects work harmoniously together. During the thirty-nine years since my father died I have tried to do two things: first, to make the lives of those who live at Chatsworth as rewarding as I can, and second, to preserve the beauty and amenities of Chatsworth, its garden and its park, so that they can be enjoyed by the countless numbers who visit them every year.

I like to think that above all Chatsworth is a community. The estate workforce numbers 150 and they, with their families and the pensioners, bring the numbers living on the estate to approximately 400. The villages of Edensor and Pilsley are lived in almost entirely by those working on the estate or by pensioners. The estate's presence is also strongly felt in Beeley and, to a lesser extent, in Baslow.

The workforce is divided among the old, traditional sections of an agricultural estate – the farm, the woods and the building yard – to which, through the inspiration of my wife, commercial ventures have been added. These include a farm shop, Chatsworth Carpenters, and the farmyard exhibition and adventure playground.

Over the years I have tried to improve and extend the tradition that there should be a strong social element in the lives of those working at Chatsworth, centred on the estate club. This has licensed premises, a billiard table and facilities for playing cards and other games. The club is housed in the charming red-brick building which is also the estate office and lies just outside the west entrance to the park. In front of it there has been a bowling green since 1920, and to its west is the golf course which was created at the turn of the century. During the First World War it became farm land, but in 1926 it became apparent that there was sufficient interest in the game for the course to be re-established. It is, by modern golf standards, a very modest affair – nine holes with eighteen tees – but nevertheless it is very popular. To belong is a perk for those living on the estate and it is run by a committee, who from time to time invite those who are good friends of Chatsworth to join.

So much for the estate. I said earlier that my other task was to preserve and improve the amenities of Chatsworth for those visiting it. This task also incorporates the interests of those who live here, so there is common ground between those who visit and those who live and work at Chatsworth.

The park covers 1,000 acres and is dominated by the house. However, visitors will also see a curious, moated, stone construction immediately on the left of the bridge as they approach the house. This dates back to the Elizabethan house built by Bess of Hardwick, of which nothing can now be seen. Bess's fourth husband was Lord Shrewsbury, who was appointed gaoler of Mary, Queen of Scots, and where he went she had to accompany him. The story goes that this Bower was built so that she could have some seclusion in fine weather, but the castellation and moat were added to preclude the possibility of her escape.

The tower on the top of the hill to the north of the house also dates from Bess's time. It consists of one room on each of its three floors. Legend has it that its original purpose was to provide a viewpoint for Bess to watch the hounds hunting deer in the park after she had become too old to be active in the chase herself. It is about to be modernized to provide living accommodation.

Two herds of deer still roam the park, one of red deer and the

other of fallow. Both breeds are shy creatures and tend to confine themselves to the remote areas during those months when the house is open to the public.

The eighteenth-century architect James Paine was responsible for the bridge which provides the main approach to the house and for the magnificent stables to its north-east. In the near future my wife intends to increase greatly the catering facilities, and where better than in this lovely building with its extraordinary rusticated stone. It will provide a suitable resting place for those who have explored the house and garden, where they can take refreshment before possibly embarking on the delights of a walk in the woods.

My wife and I have tried to meet the ever-increasing popularity of walking by cutting walks in the woods at the back of the house. These lead to tracks which run round the three big lakes that lie on a shelf of land between the woods and the moor. An area at the extreme south end of the park is set aside as a car park, for which no charge is made, so that people can leave their cars and walk virtually anywhere throughout the year. Many people love these walks, and I hope and think they appreciate that cars are not allowed.

Under the inspiration of my wife, two highly successful shops have been established. One is in the Orangery, which is the last room through which the visitors pass at the end of their tour of the house before going into the garden, and stocks a wide variety of gifts, books and souvenirs. The other is a smaller shop outside where visitors can purchase plants and produce from the garden here. In 1977 my wife introduced the farm shop in Pilsley, which sells all kinds of produce, much of it coming from the estate. Under her guidance it has become immensely successful, and is visited not only by those living locally but by people from many miles away. In the same building, built originally as a Shire horse stud, are workshops occupied by craftsmen making pottery, picture frames, curtains, fabrics and so on. These have proved so successful that an agricultural barn on the other side of the road has been converted to meet the ever-increasing demand for these various wares.

In spite of the success of these commercial ventures, Chatsworth remains essentially an oasis of rural tranquillity. It is because of this peace that so many people living in the great industrial conurbations of the north-west visit Chatsworth in their hundreds of thousands, year in and year out. It is not surprising. Search the world and you will not find a more beautiful place – I, who live here, remind myself of this every dawn and dusk, and I count myself among the most fortunate of men.

Illustrations

PALACE HOVSE. BEAVLIEV

NORTH ELEVATION

BEAULIEU

•

*The Cistercian Abbey of Beaulieu, founded in 1204, was acquired by
Sir Thomas Wriothesley, 1st Earl of Southampton, in 1738. The manor
passed later by descent to the Dukes of Montagu and Buccleuch. The house
was rebuilt in 1871 by Sir Arthur Blomfield for the 1st Lord Montagu of
Beaulieu. The estate covers 8,000 acres.*

Introduction by Lord Montagu of Beaulieu

Palace House, with its three distinctive architectural styles – monastic, fortified French manor house and Scots baronial – may not be the grandest of stately homes but it is, and has been, very much a family home. For over 400 years the Wriothesleys, Scotts and Montagus have cared lovingly for the 8,000 acres of New Forest countryside and its historic buildings, and it has been my privilege to continue this tradition.

Originally Palace House was the Great Gatehouse of Beaulieu Abbey, founded in 1204 when King John made a gift of land here to the Cistercian monks. The monastic origins of the house are evident in its architecture, particularly in the upper drawing room, one of the Abbey's chapels. This room still retains an atmosphere of tranquillity, and even today visitors sometimes remark on the smell of burning incense and the sound of Gregorian chanting. The lower drawing room as it is today did not exist then, as its present position formed in those days the pedestrian and carriage access into the Abbey through two archways to reach an inner courtyard. It was here that the Abbot would receive his guests before taking them upstairs to one of the two chapels.

In 1538 Beaulieu Abbey was dissolved and the religious buildings were destroyed beyond the possibility of restoration. The church, as the spiritual centre of the Abbey, was first to be demolished, closely followed by the cloisters and chapter-house. Some buildings which could be put to secular use were allowed to remain. As a result the monks' refectory, today the parish church of Beaulieu, and the lay brothers' dormitory, the Domus, are virtually intact. The stone and lead from the Abbey were used to build three defensive castles on the Solent, at Hurst, Calshot and Cowes, as protection against the threat of invasion from France in the 1540s.

In 1538 Beaulieu passed into the ownership of my ancestor, Thomas Wriothesley, 1st Earl of Southampton, Lord Chancellor to Henry VIII. He purchased the estate for £1,340 6s 8d, and the Great Gatehouse was turned into a residence.

During the seventeenth century Beaulieu was owned by Henry, 3rd Earl of Southampton, a courtier to Elizabeth I and later to James I. Henry spent large sums of money on the patronage of writers, among them William Shakespeare. Like his father, Henry was imprisoned in the Tower of London for his part in the Earl of Essex's plot of 1601, and was saved from execution only 'on account of his youthful good looks'. James I and his son Charles I paid frequent visits to Beaulieu for sport and hunting. On one particular visit by James in 1613 it is recorded that he was entertained by a game of football – the first royal command performance of the game ever recorded!

When Thomas, 4th Earl of Southampton, died in 1667 leaving no male heir, lots were drawn by his three daughters to see who should inherit his estates. Beaulieu was drawn by the youngest, Elizabeth, who married Ralph Montagu, while her older sister, who was married to the owner of Woburn, the Duke of Bedford, received Bloomsbury, the family

property in London. Elizabeth and Ralph's son, John, 2nd Duke of Montagu, is one of the most interesting and eccentric of my ancestors and has certainly provided my family with some wonderful anecdotes. His mother-in-law, Sarah, Duchess of Marlborough, never quite approved of his life-long love of practical jokes, which included water-pistols, itching powders and apple-pie beds. John even fortified Palace House against possible invasion by the French! Two of the four turrets which he had built survive today, together with crenellation and a moat which, because it is sited above sea-level, has never been filled with water. It has, however, yielded many interesting objects over the years, including an eighteenth-century pewter dinner service.

The Scotts inherited the Beaulieu estate through marriage in the late eighteenth century. Through the male line I can trace my ancestors back to the House of Stuart via the Duke of Monmouth, natural son of Charles II and Lucy Walters, who married Anne, Countess of Buccleuch and was created Duke of Buccleuch. Family tradition has it that my great-grandfather, 5th Duke of Buccleuch, discovered James's parents' marriage certificate which, had he produced it, would have given him a claim to the British throne. Instead, as proof of his loyalty, he showed it to Queen Victoria and then threw it into the fireplace.

My grandfather, Henry, 1st Baron Montagu of Beaulieu, was given the estate as a wedding gift in 1865. He decided it was too small for his needs, however, and almost immediately set about extending it. Correspondence with Sir Arthur Blomfield, the architect, reveals that before work could commence a large area of river mud had to be stabilized.

The estate survived the problems of two World Wars and the Depression of the 1930s, and when I inherited it on my twenty-fifth birthday in 1951, I took the decision to share my family home with the public. The Abbey ruins and grounds had in fact been open since the turn of the century, and today still constitute a major attraction for visitors. I still remember the feverish activity upon which I embarked to get everything ready for the official opening in April 1952. As a tribute to my father, John, 2nd Baron Montagu of Beaulieu, MP for the New Forest and champion of the motorists' cause in Parliament, I put five veteran cars on display in the entrance hall of the house. It was from these small beginnings that today's National Motor Museum at Beaulieu has grown.

Today, Palace House is set in an informal framework of lawns and shrub borders, shaded by mature trees. The meandering path beside the millpond is particularly pleasant on a summer's day. This design for the garden is largely of twentieth-century origin, however, and in previous centuries each generation of my family, and the Cistercian monks before them, have shaped and reshaped the land to serve their own needs and interests. From 1867 onwards my grandfather remodelled the gardens in the Victorian manner, and I plan to recreate such a garden in the future.

Sharing my home and welcoming visitors to Beaulieu has been a source of great pleasure to me. Because of our visitors Palace House, Beaulieu Abbey and the other historic buildings in my care are in a better state of repair now than they have been for many decades.

Over 800 years ago Beaulieu was christened 'the beautiful place', and it is my wish that it will always live up to its name.

Illustrations

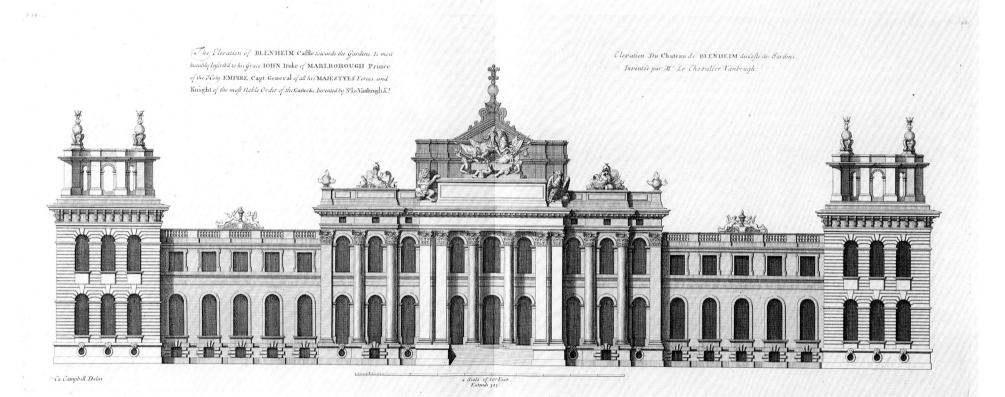

The Elevation of BLENHEIM Castle towards the Gardens. Is most humbly Inscrib'd to his Grace IOHN Duke of MARLBOROUGH Prince of the Holy EMPIRE, Capt: General of all his MAJESTYES Forces, and Knight of the most Noble Order of the Garter &c. Invented by St Io: Vanbrugh K!

Elevation Du Chateau de BLENHEIM du Costé des Iardins. Inventée par M! Le Chevalier Vanbrugh.

C: Campbell Delin:

a Scale of 100 Feet.
Extends 333.

BLENHEIM PALACE

•

Blenheim Palace is the home of the 11th Duke of Marlborough and the birthplace of Winston Churchill. It was built between the years 1705 and 1722 by Sir John Vanbrugh. The royal manor of Woodstock and the sum of £240,000 to build the palace were given to John Churchill, 1st Duke of Marlborough, by a munificent sovereign and a grateful nation in recognition of his great victory at the Battle of Blenheim in 1704. The park of 2,100 acres was landscaped by Lancelot 'Capability' Brown. The palace is at Woodstock, eight miles north of Oxford.

Introduction by the Duke of Marlborough

Blenheim has always provoked strong feelings, but as a monument to my great ancestor, John Churchill, 1st Duke of Marlborough, there can be no doubt that it manifests the awesome magnificence it was intended to inspire.

Many things have been written about Blenheim since the early eighteenth century, and many members of my family have held varying views about it, but in my mind there can be only a sense of pride in living and working in this vast palace – which is also a home – where my family has lived continuously for eleven generations.

My wife shares with me a genuine affection for Blenheim. As well as the 1st Duke, for whom Blenheim was built, the 4th Duke and the 9th Duke, my grandfather, devoted much of their lives to beautifying the palace and its grounds, many of the results of which we still enjoy today. Unfortunately there were also those among my ancestors who discarded and dispersed some treasures. The history of Blenheim and its inhabitants is as varied as an artist's palette.

It is, however, extraordinary that this diverse family holds in its fold two giants of our history: the 1st Duke, the great soldier, and Winston Churchill, my grandfather's first cousin and my godfather.

Blenheim today is fundamentally a commercial enterprise. It depends to a large degree on its visitors, without whom it would be impossible to meet the enormous costs of maintaining the palace and its grounds, and of restoring the roofs and stonework. The estate covers 11,500 acres, of which we farm 4,000. Running as a commercial operation, Blenheim is divided into five main departments – palace administration, farms, gardens, forestry, and game – each managed by its own executive head.

Major projects will have to be undertaken in the future. Rewiring the palace and dredging the lake are serious problems, and new ideas for fund-raising must constantly be considered. I have been involved in the management of the estate since 1960, and took over in 1972, on my father's death. There have been many changes over the years and I have found it a great challenge to try to bring Blenheim into the twentieth century. We hold a large number of charity events every year, and feel closely connected with the traditions of country life.

George III, approaching Blenheim through the narrow streets of Woodstock and through Woodstock Gate, is said to have exclaimed upon seeing the vast expanse of the park, lake, bridge and palace: 'We have nothing to equal this.' The view has often been described as the finest in England.

Although Blenheim was given to my ancestor and is still owned by my family, my role today is virtually that of a trustee and a custodian. I am determined to keep the estate going, not only for my family but also for future generations to enjoy, as part of the heritage of Britain and for those in every part of the world who cherish the historical tradition that Blenheim represents.

Illustrations

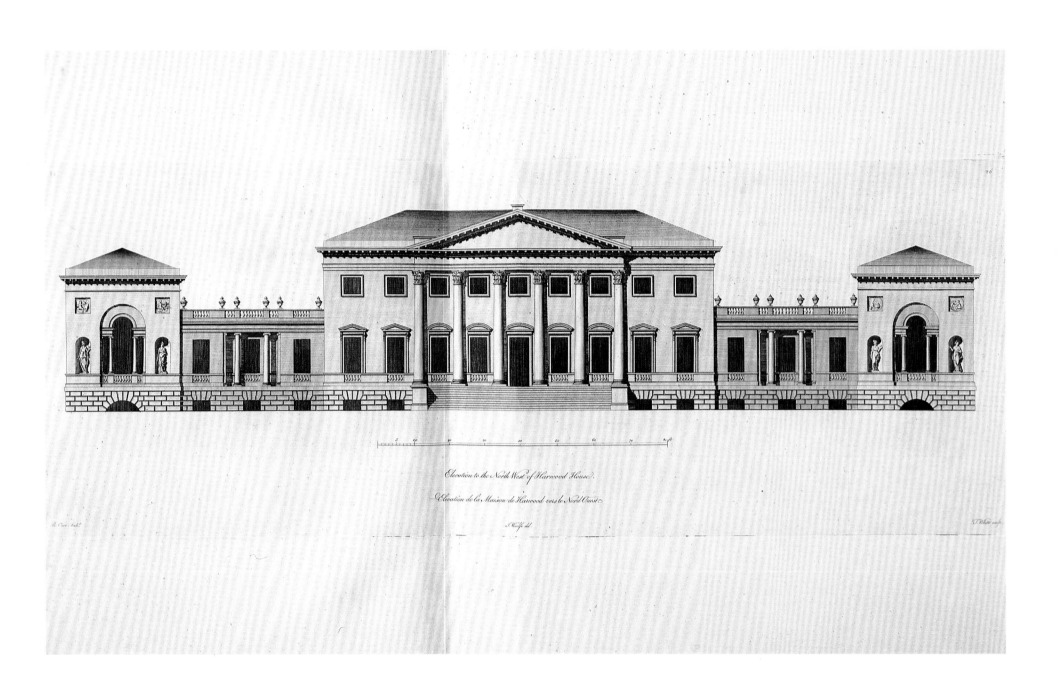

Elevation to the North West of Harwood House.

Elevation de la Maison de Harwood vers le Nord Ouest.

R. Carr Arch.t   I. Wolffe del.   G.I. White sculp.

HAREWOOD HOUSE

•

Harewood House is eight miles from Leeds in West Yorkshire, and is the ancestral home of the Earls of Harewood. It was built for Edwin Lascelles, later 1st Lord Harewood, to a Palladian design by John Carr of York in 1759; Robert Adam was concerned with the final product, which was enlarged by Sir Charles Barry in 1845. The gardens were landscaped by Lancelot 'Capability' Brown in 1772 and the park covers 1,500 acres.

Introduction by the Earl of Harewood

My family first lived at Harewood in 1771, and the earliest visitors came the following year. In increasing numbers they have continued to come ever since, until by the later 1960s, when we started to open to the public on a professional basis – to earn part of the cost of upkeep – they were averaging more than ¼ million a year. I have always had a horror of watching any part of this house start to atrophy, by which I mean being enjoyed neither by family nor by public and so acquiring the kind of musty smell found in buildings after disuse – summerhouses and cricket pavilions at the end of winter, war-time storage places when peace came. Emphasis on how the house contributes may have changed over two centuries, but it was intended to be used by quite a large number of people and that I am convinced is how it should be today, just as when it was first occupied.

Edwin Lascelles, who built and established Harewood as an eighteenth-century centre of activity, went to Robert Adam for its interior design, to Chippendale for its furniture and decoration, to Reynolds to paint his stepdaughters and himself, and to 'Capability' Brown for the landscape. The results of his commissions and taste are to this day all over the house and park and a main reason why people come to look at Harewood.

But Edwin did not only build a house, he owned and ran an estate. In 1795, after his death, a meticulous inventory was made including a detailed list of horses, cattle and sheep, farm implements and so on, and through the years the various aspects of agricultural life were very much in evidence at Harewood – flowers, a big 'kitchen' garden, forestry, control of predators through game-keeping, and of course farming. The park was ploughed up during both World Wars, my father in his time re-started forestry, to which my grandfather had seemed allergic, but we had twin setbacks in the early 1960s when foot-and-mouth disease struck one side of productivity, and from another on successive days freak gales took out 10,000 old trees and 20,000 new. Forestry continues as a main activity, with the old cycle of cutting and replanting, to which one must add a regular effort to replace 200-year-old trees which formed a main part of 'Capability' Brown's plan. Something new is the breeding of rare birds in the Harewood Bird Garden, which revives an eighteenth-century enthusiasm.

In Edwin Lascelles's day, judging by the inventory, everything was new and nothing seems to have been transferred from the old house (called Gawthorpe and situated at the bottom of the hill, near the stream which feeds the lake) where his father lived and where he had been

seventy-nine

brought up. I sometimes wonder what was on the walls at Gawthorpe, and, if it was pictures, what Edwin did with them after the move. At Harewood, the inventory suggests that it was the product of Chippendale's fertile imagination which provided the inhabitants with incident to delight the eye rather than pictures, of which there were relatively few. The grand rooms were full of mirrors and girandoles, of console tables and highly decorated chairs, and the mirrors with their reflections must have made the rooms remarkably light by day and by night.

Succeeding generations have left their mark. Edwin's cousin Edward Lascelles, who inherited from him, also patronized Reynolds, adding Hoppner the portrait painter to his list; but his eldest son (who died before his father) was Harewood's first real collector. He was a friend of Turner and Girtin, whom he commissioned, and a connoisseur of French china, which led him to buy Sèvres and Chinese celadon in Paris in 1803 after the Peace of Amiens. The next generation was content to represent North Yorkshire in Parliament, but the 3rd Earl, who was wounded at the Battle of Waterloo in 1815, married Louisa Thynne from Longleat, and whether because of their family of thirteen or simply to emulate her father's much bigger house, she set about enlarging what she had inherited, adding a bedroom storey at either end of the house and in the middle and placing the house itself firmly on a terrace, which turned it from a grand English country house into something like an Italian palace.

That was perhaps a demonstration of period and of aspiration above those of her husband's forebears, but what is interesting is that the redecoration of the much altered house also involved a wholesale replacement of the grand Chippendale mirrors and tables, some of which were carefully packed away and stored, and also the removal of much of the filigree ornament with which Chippendale had adorned his creations. The Victorians, contrary to common belief, wanted it simpler. After Louisa the next major influence was my father, who looked after Harewood from 1929 to 1947, and he inherited Canning and Clanricarde collections as well as buying major Italian pictures for Harewood where before there had been none.

Much furniture was restored before 1939, but a recent and more inquisitive outlook has now revealed that what were previously thought to be cases of derelict and unusable pieces stored at the back of the joiner's shop contained pairs to what we had thought were single mirrors, as well as a further and wonderfully ornate pair we had presumed lost. How to accommodate what we found and are restoring in rooms which have assumed over a couple of generations a form of their own, and which are full not only of furniture but of pictures never envisaged in Chippendale's time, poses a problem whose solution may produce some further changes in this old house.

Activity looks likely to keep at bay the mustiness I learned to dread. We have maintained and even extended the collection of rhododendrons my parents enjoyed importing to Yorkshire, and computerization is helping us to make both their botanical and their historical details more easily accessible to the public. Events seem to range from associations that go easily with the countryside, like horses and dogs, to those with slightly remoter connections, like steam engines and cars, but perhaps the most enjoyable of all has been the hosting a year or two ago of the Game Fair. Looking out of the window in the morning to see rows of tents all over the South Park was to be reminded of the encampment before the Battle of Agincourt in the film of *Henry V.* Edwin Lascelles would doubtless have dispatched a furious memo to his agent complaining of damage to the grazing. But because he liked what was new, he might have enjoyed it just the same.

Illustrations

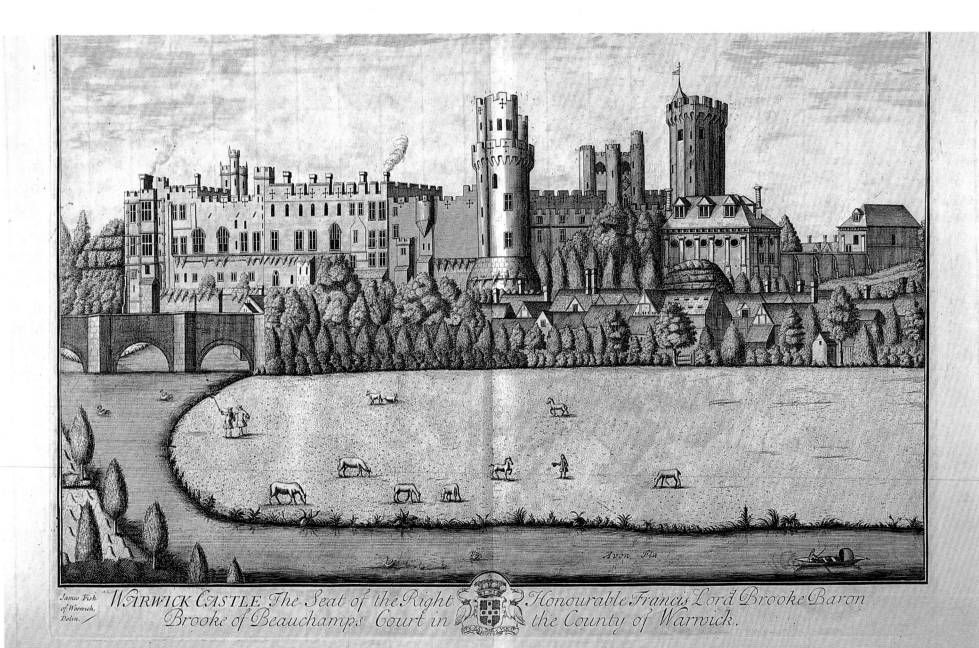

James Fish
of Warwick,
Delin.

WARWICK CASTLE *The Seat of the Right* Honourable Francis Lord Brooke Baron Brooke of Beauchamps Court in the County of Warwick.

Avon Fla

WARWICK CASTLE

•

In 1068 William the Conqueror ordered the building of the castle at Warwick on the banks of the River Avon. It was later developed into a mighty stronghold by the de Beauchamp family and afterwards a grand mansion. In 1604 James I granted the castle to the Greville family who became Barons Brooke and later Earls of Warwick. Warwick Castle was sold by the present Earl of Warwick to The Tussauds Group in 1978.

Introduction by Michael Herbert

In all England there is nothing quite like Warwick Castle, the annals of which begin in Saxon times. Though sacked, besieged and seriously damaged by fire throughout its long history, the castle remains the noblest and most picturesque of our surviving ancient fortresses. On a visit in 1828 Sir Walter Scott, the great romantic novelist, described it as 'that fairest monument of ancient and chivalrous splendour that yet remains uninjured by time'.

The Saxon chronicles tell us that Ethelfleda, the daughter of King Alfred the Great, fortified many towns bordering her realm of Mercia, including the ancient town of Warwick. It is certainly probable that her programme of fortifications in 914 extended to the present site of the castle, commanding the vital river crossing. Certainly William the Conqueror recognized the strategic importance of the site, and ordered one of the first castles in the country to be built in 1068 as he advanced up country to quell rebellion in the north of England.

When his son, William II, came to the throne in 1088 the castle was granted to Henry de Newburgh and he also acquired the earldom of Warwick. A stone castle began to be built from this period onwards, until in 1264, during the Barons' War, forces under the command of John Giffard sallied forth from nearby Kenilworth Castle, one of Simon de Montfort's strongholds, sacked the castle and carried off the Earl and Countess, who were subsequently ransomed.

The castle now passed into the hands of one of the most illustrious families, the Beauchamps, who held the castle well into the mid-fifteenth century. Immensely wealthy and made rich by services to the Crown during the Hundred Years War with France, they began a protracted building programme throughout the fourteenth century, each son following the work of his father until they had achieved the construction of a castle which incorporated the very best contemporary designs in military architecture. As so often happened with the great families of the Middle Ages (and the Beauchamps are remarkable for their longevity in this respect), no direct male heir was forthcoming in the mid-fifteenth century and the remaining heiress, Anne Beauchamp, married Richard Neville, later to become Earl of Salisbury as well as Earl of Warwick. Neville, who has been styled 'the last of the Barons', was a major influence throughout the Wars of the Roses. He imprisoned Edward IV for a short time at Warwick Castle and also held Henry VI in the Tower of London. He changed sides more than once during the conflict, and after fleeing to

France he returned only to be defeated by Edward IV at the Battle of Barnet in 1471, at which he was killed. The name of Warwick had become a powerful symbol and rallying point for the forces of dissension. Thus the castle passed into the hands of the Crown and the earldom lapsed.

After Neville's death the Duke of Clarence held the castle for the King, his elder brother Edward IV, but Clarence was drowned in a butt of Malmsey wine in 1478 in the Tower of London, some say at the hand of his younger brother Richard, Duke of Gloucester, later King Richard III, who now became the owner of Warwick Castle and began work on a massive artillery fort, the remains of which can still be seen to this day.

With the death of King Richard at the Battle of Bosworth in 1485, the building work ceased and the castle became Crown property.

Henry VIII, it is known, did a considerable amount of strengthening work, underpinning and rebuilding part of the massive river front. It was during his reign that the castle was granted to the Dudley family, who had quickly risen through the ranks as administrators for Henry VII, but they too fell foul of the Crown in their attempt to put Lady Jane Grey on the throne.

Under Queen Elizabeth, Ambrose Dudley, who had been attainted, regained the title and the castle, and he died without issue in 1590 from wounds received fighting the Queen's wars. The castle once again became Crown property and, for a time at least, was the county gaol.

In 1603 Sir Fulke Greville, a wealthy wool merchant from the Cotswolds, successfully petitioned James I and was granted Warwick Castle. He subsequently spent £20,000, an enormous sum in those days, undertaking its restoration. It was he who began the massive task of converting an otherwise stark fortress into a magnificent mansion befitting a man of importance. Greville had been Treasurer of the Navy under Elizabeth I and was a Privy Councillor to James I. He was murdered in London in 1628, and his body was brought back to Warwick and buried in a great tomb in the Chapter House of St Mary's Church.

His successor, Robert Greville, supported the parliamentary cause against the King and was Commander of the Militia in Warwickshire and Staffordshire. In 1642 the castle was besieged by Royalist forces under the command of the Marquess of Northampton, but it held out for fourteen days, Robert Greville, Lord Brooke, bringing his troops from Banbury to drive off the besiegers. Throughout the Civil War and in spite of the death of Robert Greville, who was killed by a sniper from the top of Lichfield Cathedral in 1643, the castle was a parliamentarian stronghold and of some strategic importance. Ironically, however, it was Robert's second

son who was instrumental in helping to restore Charles II to the throne in 1660, and it was from this point that the castle interiors start to take the shape which we see to this day, following on from the work which had been begun by Sir Fulke Greville.

About this time also the acquisition of the fine collections of paintings and furniture began to adorn the remodelled state rooms.

By the eighteenth century the castle had become firmly established in the hands of the Greville family, who acquired the title of Earl of Warwick in 1759. Francis Greville successfully petitioned the King for the title, which had become vacant when the Rich family, who had achieved pre-eminence during the late seventeenth century, died out.

It was Francis Greville who gave the famous English landscape gardener Lancelot ('Capability') Brown his first commission to beautify the castle grounds while Brown was still employed at Stowe. Brown's influence at Warwick Castle is still very apparent today. Many of his fine plantings survive, most notably some large oaks and cedars of Lebanon.

With such an important history, what is remarkable about Warwick Castle is the fact that it has survived virtually intact. Additions have been made, restoration has taken place and indeed half of the interiors were remodelled after the great fire in 1871, but in spite of this the building in its superb setting conjures up a vision of the romance of the Middle Ages and to that extent fulfils most people's ideas of what a mediaeval castle should be.

Set in gracious parkland by Shakespeare's Avon, the castle is a delight to visit at all seasons of the year, and although its illustrious owners through the centuries have all faded away, this great and remarkable building survives as a living testament.

Since 1978 the castle has been owned by The Tussauds Group, part of Pearson plc.

Illustrations

Broadlands

N.C.H. Nisbett
March

BROADLANDS

•

Broadlands is the home of Lord Romsey, grandson and heir of the Earl Mountbatten of Burma. The beautiful Palladian house is situated next to the town of Romsey in Hampshire.

Introduction by Lord Romsey

For a large landed estate which has passed through many generations, it is remarkable that Broadlands has remained virtually the same since its establishment long before the Norman Conquest.

The estate was originally part of the Romsey Abbey lands, and on the present site of the house stood the main farmhouse, which was later altered in the Jacobean manner. In 1736 the estate was acquired by my ancestor the 1st Viscount Palmerston, a Minister of the Navy after whom Palmerston Island in the South Seas is named. His son, the 2nd Viscount Palmerston, after his 'grand tour' of Europe, decided to convert the Jacobean mansion into the beautiful classical Palladian house we see today. The transformation began in 1767 with the help of Lancelot 'Capability' Brown and Henry Holland. Palmerston acquired an important collection of sculpture and paintings, and had much of the existing furniture specially built for the house. The Broadlands of 1989 remains one of the finest examples of mid-Georgian architecture in Britain.

The 3rd Lord Palmerston, the famous prime minister, grandson of the 2nd Viscount, inherited the house in 1802. With his marriage to his great love Emily Lamb, widow of the Earl Cowper, the estate passed down to the Ashleys through the Shaftesbury part of the family and thence to my grandmother, Edwina, who married my grandfather, the Earl Mountbatten of Burma.

Prime Minister Palmerston and Lord Mountbatten are two members of the family who stand out as great individuals of English history who also, even in their busy lives, found time to devote to Broadlands. Lord Palmerston often rode from the Palace of Westminster to Broadlands in seven or eight hours with frequent changes of horse. Not surprisingly, he welcomed the arrival of the railway at Romsey! The wives of both men also dearly loved Broadlands. Lady Palmerston wrote: 'Nothing can be more comfortable than this House. It is magnificent when we have company and when alone it seems to be only a Cottage in a beautiful garden.' It is not only the owners who have felt this – countless visitors to Broadlands have testified as much over the centuries, from statesmen, artists, writers, to members of most of Europe's royal families, many of whom still visit today. Lord Mountbatten's nephew, the Duke of Edinburgh, and Her Majesty The Queen chose Broadlands as their honeymoon retreat in 1947, as did the Prince and Princess of Wales in 1981.

Lord Mountbatten decided to share his delight in Broadlands with a wider array of visitors when he opened the house to the public in 1979.

one hundred and nine

In return, these visitors contributed in large measure to the continued existence of the house, for both it and the adjacent buildings need enormous funds for vital restoration and maintenance work. Tragically, my grandfather was assassinated by the IRA in August of the same year, but he had enjoyed the preparation and the early weeks of opening. He was frequently to be seen going out personally to greet the visitors, who were surprised and delighted to meet this famous man face to face.

So when my turn came to take over Broadlands, I was determined to continue his wishes. Since childhood, I had always looked forward with excitement and pleasure to family visits there, and had got to know the families living on the estate – along with the staff in the house – who are the essence of Broadlands. For hundreds of years the estate had comprised the house, the gardens, the farms, the river, the game and the forestry, and I realized the necessity of trying to make each department financially self-sufficient in this increasingly commercial and competitive world if it was to survive. So with my wife and all those who work at Broadlands, I set about the task.

We offer added enjoyment to those visiting the house and gardens with an exhibition dedicated to the lives of my grandparents, and with amenities such as a restaurant and a shop. We have expanded and invested in the farm, and are currently planning to sell produce directly to the public. The forestry department encompasses commercial planting, hardwood planting for the sake of the environment, and a maintenance plan following 'Capability' Brown's design for the park, for the benefit of future generations. The shooting is a thriving business, and as well as three and a half miles of fishing on the famous salmon and trout river Test, we have developed the two lakes for the coarse fisherman. In addition, the estate supports numerous charity events and country organizations.

It is a challenge to develop and modernize the different elements of the estate today, in order to preserve the very character of the land, buildings and life as they were over 200 years ago. This is not just for myself or only for those loyal people who live and work here, but for those hundreds of thousands who visit Broadlands, and for the greater community around us which passes through the estate daily. Indeed, I was brought up to believe that I only hold Broadlands in trust for future generations.

Lord Palmerston said: 'This place pleases me above any place I know.' My family and the estate have worked towards this end and I count myself fortunate to be able to repeat his words, which many of my forebears have echoed. I hope only that many other people will be able to join me in saying the same for a very long time to come.

Illustrations

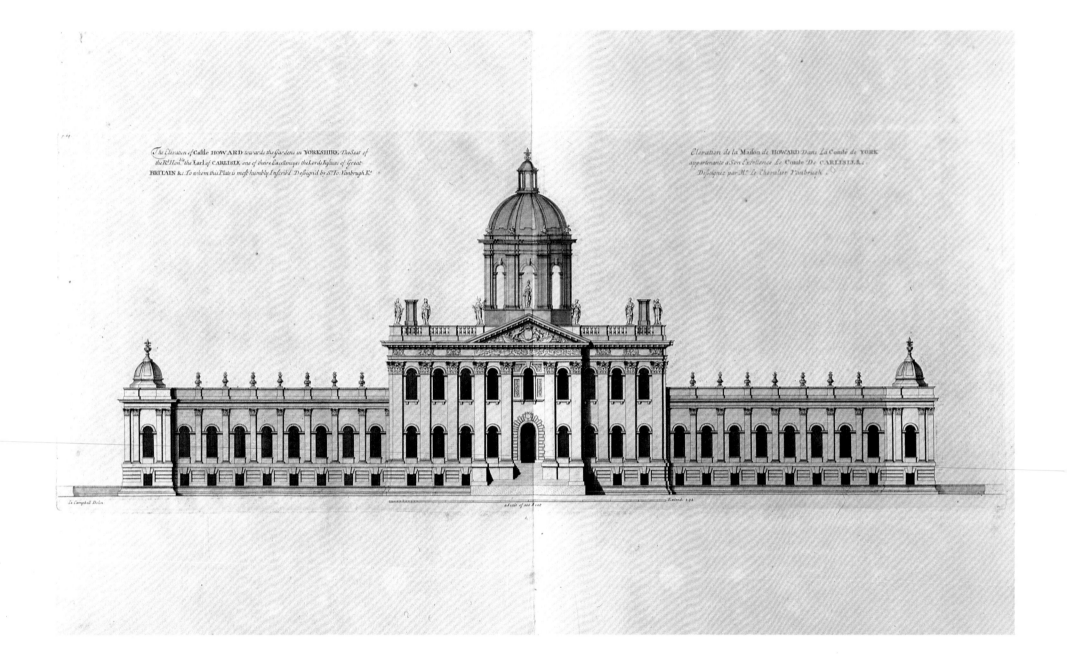

The Elevation of Castle HOWARD towards the Gardens in YORKSHIRE, The Seat of the R.t Hon.ble the Earl of CARLISLE, one of theire Excellencys the Lords Justices of Great BRITAIN &.c To whom this Plate is most humbly Inscrib'd Design'd by S.r Jo. Vanbrugh K.t

Elevation de la Maison de HOWARD Dans La Comté de YORK appartenante a Son Excellence Le Comte De CARLISLE &.c Desseigné par M.r le Chevalier Vanbrugh &.c

Co: Campbell Delin:

a Scale of 100 Feet

Fourdri: Sculp:

CASTLE HOWARD

•

Castle Howard, fifteen miles east of York, is the home of the Hon. Simon Howard, descendant of the Dukes of Norfolk and of the 3rd Earl of Carlisle, for whom Sir John Vanbrugh, assisted by Nicholas Hawksmoor, built the huge house from 1699 onwards. The building was completed by Sir Thomas Robinson in the mid-eighteenth century. The estate, covering 10,000 acres, contains temples, pyramids, obelisks and Hawksmoor's splendid mausoleum.

Introduction by the Hon. Simon Howard

'Nobody had informed me that at one view I should see a palace, a town, a fortified city, temples on high places, woods worthy of being each a metropolis of the Druids, the noblest lawn in the world fenced by half the horizon, and a mausoleum that would tempt one to be buried alive, in short, I have seen gigantic palaces before, but never a sublime one.'

These words, committed for posterity by Horace Walpole, still reflect the immense surprise that greets one when visiting Castle Howard even today. Its sheer scale of design leaves people in awe of a time when grand visions were executed in the grand manner. But much more of a surprise is that it is still home to the same family who were responsible for its creation, and that ever since that creation it has been open to the visitor up to and including the present day.

The house was built by Charles Howard, 3rd Earl of Carlisle, a man of immense power, ambition, vanity and self-esteem. At that time there were a considerable number of grand country houses being constructed and, although it would be wrong to suggest that Carlisle was simply trying to outdo his contemporaries, there can be no doubt that the country seat was the most flamboyant of status symbols. The building of the house was surrounded by controversy from the beginning. Learned men of the day denounced it as being neither one style nor the other because of the flagrant mixture of orders, rustications and superimposed detail. Even after the completion of the building of the house by the 4th Earl, his son the 5th Earl was to write: 'One of the things most difficult for any of us to comprehend was my father's building of the new wing at Castle Howard. Sir Thomas Robinson, whom he laughed at, by perpetual teasing carried his point, and my father gave way when his faculties had no appearance of being weakened. He lived long enough to be disgusted with all its uncomparable faults.' It was not until the late-nineteenth century, at the time of the 8th Earl, that the trustees carried out the extensive alterations which harmonized the symmetry of the appearance of the house. On 9 November 1940, unfortunately, two-thirds of the south front and the entire dome were destroyed by fire. They were restored in 1960 by George Howard, later Lord Howard of Henderskelfe, and in the 1980s further restoration has continued.

The restoration of the house is reflected in the work that has been carried out throughout the grounds and estate. Ever since the original conception of the house, the grounds have been a very important feature, displaying not only the enormous collections of flora and fauna, but also the rich variety of architectural follies that litter the landscape in such precise orders and manners. While a large lake dominates the northern views to the house, there are a series of fountains, small lakes, cascades and waterfalls that meander their way through hidden gardens to the south. These, which started life as small ponds, were progressively improved until eventually the latter part of the nineteenth century saw them built up to their grandest. Sadly, because certain volumes and flow measures were not understood then, the lakes and other works fell into disrepair. Now, however, with our twentieth-century knowledge, we have been able to resurrect these and once again show them off to their former glory.

It is interesting to note that, like most families in grand country houses in England, the Carlisles had their fair share both of misfortune and of good luck. It was the 5th Earl who managed, through excessive gambling, to lose most of the family estates and create immense debts which were felt long after his death. That was one side of the coin, however; he also managed to collect a great many of the magnificent paintings which now hang not only in Castle Howard but also in our national museums. The 9th Earl of Carlisle was among those responsible for the latter because, in his role as a trustee of the National Gallery, he felt obliged to donate certain works of art to the nation. His wife, after the 9th Earl's death, donated others.

Today Castle Howard is still the home of the Howard family, although many would have you believe that the Marchmains of Brideshead live here. Indeed, such is the power of television that members of the public often inquire whether Sebastian is still drinking as much!

In this increasingly competitive age, Castle Howard has continued to evolve in many areas and ways in order that it may survive. In attracting certain financially rewarding events, even the Carlisle family motto, *Volo Non Valeo,* has suffered at the mouth of the visitor; on espying the said motto, a member of the public was overheard to say, when asked by a member of his party where the money came from to build Castle Howard, 'Well, judging by what's written up there, Volvo must have provided it!'

Our family have always regarded Castle Howard as home, even to the extent of riding bicycles round the corridors as children – a fact that I am sure would terrify the conservationists of today – but it is the devotion and love which has been shown to the estate over the years that has made it live, and it is the continuation of that love that will account for its survival.

Illustrations

Acknowledgements

In 1987, Beesley Gibbons Ltd gained permission from the Treasure Houses Group to produce a hardback book reflecting the glory of the great estates of Britain. It was the culmination of months of detailed preparation and planning.

The book is primarily a visual experience, not only taking the reader on a tour of these great estates but also going behind the scenes to areas seldom visited by the public. This could not have been achieved without the full co-operation of the owners, estate administrators and staff, to whom we would like to extend our sincere thanks for their patience (even at the crack of dawn) and their understanding of the problems we experienced in the compiling of the book.

The splendour of **The Treasure Houses of England** was captured by using the very latest development in photographic technology from Linhof, the Master Technika 5 x 4, and the Technorama 617S, a new piece of equipment which produces a high resolution transparency measuring 60mm x 170mm. Even more important was the technical service and location back-up extended to us by Paula Pell-Johnson and her team at Linhof Professional Sales, London, and by Horst Hensel of Linhof in Germany.

We felt strongly that the production standards of the book should reflect the grandeur of the subject matter. The processing of the film and the colour separation had to be completed with the utmost accuracy. Those involved in this side of the reproduction were first Joey and Paul Simms at Colourbox, Oxford, who processed our film, more often than not at a moment's notice, always to the same high standard, and second Les Lett and everyone at Culver Graphics, High Wycombe, who put up with us camping out on their doorstep while the technical work was in progress. We extend our thanks to them all.

     Thanks also to Eleo Gordon, our editor at Viking, who guided us through the minefield of publishing with such enthusiasm and goodwill; to Mike and Gary for their advice in the early stages of this project; to Jan Hancock, whose encouragement and hard work kept us on schedule, and who also found time to become Mrs Earl Beesley; to the Bodleian Library, Oxford, who supplied us with the illustrations on pages 7, 22, 60, 78, 94 and 128; and to all those others too numerous to mention, whose contributions helped to make this book possible. The result of all this endeavour is a book which is, quite simply, a pleasure to view.

Earl A. Beesley
Garry Gibbons